Make Up Don't Break Up

Parent Your Inner Child Before Being a Parent

Raja Mishal, PhD

This edition published by Raja Mishal 2017
Copyright © Raja Mishal, 2017
Cover design and Photography: Well Designs.
Email: well@graphic-designer.com
ISBN: 97800994921437

The right of Raja Mishal to be identified as the Author of the Work has been asserted in accordance with the Copyright, Designs and Patents Act 1988.

All rights reserved. No part of this publication may be reproduced, stored in a retrieval system, or transmitted, in any form or by any means without the prior written permission of the publisher, nor be otherwise circulated in any form of binding or cover other than that in which it is published and without a similar condition being imposed on the subsequent purchaser.

Disclaimer

This book is designed to provide insight, information, and personal empowerment to our readers to help them shift negative emotions that do not serve them anymore. It is sold with the understanding that the author is not engaged to render any type of psychological, psychiatric, or any kind of medical advice. This book is not meant to be used, nor should it be used, to diagnose or treat any medical condition. For diagnosis or treatment of any medical problem, consult your own physician. Although in this book the author describes illness and disharmony according to Chinese philosophy, the author is not rendering any diagnosis of any kind but the information in this book should be used as a guidance to expand the reader's awareness to the emotional and spiritual causes of ill health. To diagnose and treat using alternative and complementary medicine, the reader should consult a health care practitioner that is licensed to practice Chinese Medicine. The author is not responsible for any specific health that may require medical supervision and the author is not liable for any physical, psychological, or negative consequences to any person reading or following the information in this book. Our views and rights are the same: You are responsible for your own choices, actions, and results. References are provided for informational purposes only and do not constitute endorsement of any websites or other sources. Readers should be aware that the websites listed in this book may change. Some names and identifying details have been changed to protect the privacy of individuals.

Dedication

This book is dedicated to anyone who wants to be the best version of himself and to all parents who want to raise empowered children for generations to come

Contents

An Open Invitation to the Reader....................... ix

1 It All Started in the Brain 1

2 I Blame My Parents 7

3 Am I a Thinker or A Doer? 11

4 Core Emotional Blueprint Tendencies 15

5 Epigenetic Factors 27

6 Genetics, Epigenetics, and Energetics 33

7 The Fear of Losing the Circus...........................37

8 A Smiley Face and a Sad Heart 49

9 Worry Kills Intimacy 55

10 It is My Way or The Highway 63

11 Core Love Blueprint Tendencies....................73

Epilogue..85

Bibliography...89

About the Author 91

An Open Invitation to the Reader

It has been two years since I wrote my first book "Shift to Shine: Bridging Science and Intuition". When I wrote Shift to Shine it was from the perspective of introducing a new and innovative approach to dealing with stress from an energetic and spiritual point of view. Shift to Shine was about helping us connect to who we really are and be in alignment with our higher self and what are we supposed to do on earth, which is the true cause of stress. The book was based on my personal life, as well as on treating patients with Chinese Medicine during the years of my professional practice. Two years later, I sit down to write a new book, the one that you are holding in your hand right now. I was inspired and compelled to write about relationships because of what is going on today in our world of dysfunctional relationships, with both parents and children are paying a dear price.

When I started writing "Make Up Don't Break Up", I suddenly realized that my first book Shift to Shine was mainly about family relationships. I wrote extensively about my family dynamics, the culture I grew up in, and the negative emotions I and others harbored based on genetics (nature) and epigenetics (nurture) factors I connected to energetic genes. The similarities between the books are astounding because what you will read in this book is also based on genetics and epigenetics, but this time it is about how they affect our behaviour and personality which in turn will determine how we live our lives and how we communicate with the outside world.

Too many men and women start relationships and bring their emotional baggage into the new life they have planned together. Many of these relationships fail whether in its infancy or after many years of being together. While many people decide to continue being in a dysfunctional relationship, others muster the courage to leave, looking for a fresh start and new beginnings. The ones who stay in their relationships are not happy and do not represent what a family unit is about. The ones who leave their dysfunctional relationships can attract more of the same energy, and would just keep seeking the perfect match that will complete them and make them happy.

What then the message we are sending to our future generations? Is it okay to be unhappy and live a mediocracy life? Is it okay to settle for less? Or is it that we do not care much about raising emotionally healthy, empowered, and balanced children who one day will be parents? What is it that we are really teaching our children about relationships? Do we want them to lose hope in love and faith in a family unit? This is my reasoning for writing Make Up Don't Break Up. Too many relationships break up while many more make it through. **My intention is for all of us to Make it through our relationships,** enabling us to raise empowered children who will in turn raise more empowered children for generations to come.

Many of us are broken on the inside, but that does not mean we cannot fix ourselves and glue our inner wounds to be the best parents that we can be. Having wounds does not mean that we have to raise wounded children and wounded families. We can HEAL those wounds even if it was not perfect because healing takes a long time to eradicate what happened in the past. However, what is more important is that we start the healing journey. It is even critical to start healing way before we delve into a relationship or have children. When we are healed on the inside, we will attract the right person into our life who will share our vision, mission, views, and agree on what is important in the relationship and how to raise healthy, balanced children and families.

We owe it to our future generations and to ourselves to start doing so today because it will take time to shift family patterns and raise empowered children and have empowered families. Thus, I extend my hand to you to help me out in bringing awareness and healing to our relationships, so we can leave a legacy of success, love, and peace on earth. This book is an open invitation to everyone who wants to be a better parent, a better spouse, a better friend, a better caregiver, a better co-worker, a better boss, a better grandparent and in general a better person. This book is not only for parents, but more so for any human being who wants to reach their fullest potential and make an impact in the world to affect future generations.

Make Up Don't Break Up is written on the premise that we need to connect with our inner child and parent it before we bring our own children to the world. Consider what is mentioned in this book a test drive to test your ability in the future in parenting your children. I don't think anyone would buy a car without first going for a test drive, so why would you have children before taking the journey within to parent your inner child? Should you pass this preparatory test, I am confident you will be able to have amazing relationships and raise empowered children because now you are a pro at parenting. Looking after our inner child is the first step in being a parent. Neglecting the inner child will make it a lot easier to neglect our own children and family as you will learn from Malcolm's story.

In this book, you will first learn about the four different types of temperaments (traits, characteristics) and the role of genetics and epigenetics in shaping our personalities and behaviour. Then I introduce an emotional blueprint each temperament is more likely to exhibit. Our nature dictates our needs, values, fears and how we deal with emotions and stressors in our lives. This is why it is important to learn about our emotional blueprint tendencies, so that we can release those negative energies from our psyche.

Healing exercises are offered after that, which will aid in releasing those negative emotions. I am a big believer in taking baby steps when it comes to healing and shifting our lives in a new direction, and therefore I chose simple yet effective healing exercises that will help you achieve your goals.

<u>The trick here is that these exercises must be performed for few minutes daily for a period of at least one month to reap their benefits</u>.

Chinese modality healing exercises have been chosen as they are so powerful in releasing negative deep-seated emotions, hence, you may experience some negative emotions at the beginning when you start your practice. If you feel slight discomfort that is fine, however, if you feel more anger or sadness, then stop doing the exercises temporarily and give it another try in a couple of weeks. You are the best person to gauge your feelings and your behaviour. Healing cannot be forced, and if there is pain there is no gain. You need to be ready to take the new step in the new direction. Additionally, do not work on more than one emotion at the same time. Make a choice based on the strongest emotion that you are going through now and then proceed from there.

In my opinion, life is not complete without love, therefore in the last chapter I make an attempt to explain the different ways of displaying love and affection based on temperament, and offer one of the most profound healing exercises "Forgiveness" to heal any open wound. At the end of the day, you must exhibit some of the "thinker temperament" and be a detective. Listen carefully to what others around you say and how they act because they are giving you clues you need to follow to solve the relationship hiccup mystery. Listen with your heart and your Soul and be open to meet their needs and connect with them emotionally because once you do so, you would have found the secret to living a happy life, have amazing relationships, and raising wonderful children. What a treasure to keep and pass on to future generations.

Keep Shining Your Light,
With Love,

1

It All Started in the Brain

Malcolm was an angry man. Everything about him shouted anger. His stern face expressions, the way he sulks, and the way he gazes at you freezes the blood in your veins and stops the breath you take. He was angry at the world, but for most he was angry at himself. He did not have great relationships, either with his family or with people around him. People could feel the anger energy and stayed away. He ended up living lonely and died lonely. Not a single person attended his funeral, not even his own children, not because people hated him, but because he did not have a single relationship in his life. He alienated everyone including his own children, which makes one thinks what a dear price Malcolm had to pay for being a victim of his own anger.

In this day and age of body/mind/spirit philosophy, it is critical to understand the role emotions play in establishing relationships with ourselves, others, and in raising future generations. It is important to recognize that anger, fear and other negative emotions, especially those ones generated early on in life, can have devastating effects on us and on future generations if we do not heal them now. This is exactly what happened with Malcolm where his relationships with his coworkers and his family suffered the most and he ended up loosing everything.

The goal of this book is to help you heal your relationship with yourself first, then with your family, and finally with others around you in the hopes that when you start your family, you will have amazing and the most fabulous relationships with your spouse and children and leave a powerful legacy for generations to come. Relationships are probably one of the most complicated things in life to comprehend. If that is not complicated enough, wait until we get to talk about family relationships and family culture.

These days, there are many broken relationships and even many more successful ones. So, what breaks a relationship or makes it? Have you ever thought about that? Or are you one of those people who enter the relationship lottery and take his chances with it? What are the factors that determine relationship success and if you have a family, what determines your family relationship dynamics?

There are two important factors that determine if a relationship is going to make it or break it, namely genetics and epigenetics, which are established before conception. Needless to say, my training as a Molecular Geneticist and Neuroscientist has influenced my thought process and analysis of situations that deal with any type of building connections. Observation is the scientist's strongest suit. Observing how people behave in their relationships and close inspection of my own personal life and other cultures made me come to the above conclusion. Little I knew then, that twenty years later I am transferring what I learned during my doctorate research years to apply it in a family setting instead of a brain setting.

So back to our two factors, genetics and epigenetics. Genetics is what our parents pass on to us, while epigenetics is the environment you live in. In other words, there are two forces that affect your behavior: one inherited and the other environmental. The combination of the two shapes your life and determines success or failure in life in general and in relationships in particular.

I was intrigued with the idea of having two forces that work either cohesively or non-cohesively to shape the way cells make connections, the way these connections affect structures, and finally the way these structures determine the overall behavior of the organism.

In my training of Medical Neuroscience, I focused on how cells build connections, albeit at the molecular level. For my doctorate thesis research, I examined factors that determined how neurons in the sensory cortex make connections during early stages of development. Our department obtained mutant mice that had certain structures (called barrels) missing from the brain. The principal investigators I worked for were successful in securing some funding in collaboration with the department of Psychology and Neuroscience to investigate the molecular mechanisms that underlie pattern formation in the brain and how the absence of these structures affected behavior, short- and long-term memory.

Once you get into the wonderful world of the brain, you cannot be but astonished at the intricacy of what happens within it. Billions of cells must establish correct connections way before birth. Timing is of utmost importance in life and it could not be truer in this case. Certain molecules called trophic factors, which act as a guide to neurons, must be present in the environment in the right quantity and at the right time. Otherwise, neurons will either make deformed connections or will fail to make proper connections altogether.

The above is also true in the peripheral nervous system. In my post-doctoral fellowship, I investigated the connections retina neurons make by injecting them with a fluorescent dye, after which a tracer was used to examine how these neurons are coupled. I believe if two of the most complicated systems in the human body reveal that the environment dictates the type of connections they made, then we can extrapolate that to human behavior and relationships. At the time of writing my dissertation, the common dogma was to emphasise the role of genetics over epigenetics. Over the years, scientific research has proven without a shred of a doubt that both genetics and epigenetics play important roles in establishing and re-establishing neuronal connections in the brain. These findings are critical to our understanding of how the brain functions and hence, how our thoughts and behaviors are affected by this plasticity (flexibility). These results ensue a high level of optimism in the capacity of human beings adapting to the surrounding environment and modifying behaviors if we are plastic or flexible enough.

In the following chapters, we will delve into the role of genetics in creating our core temperaments and how we can modify the environment (epigenetics) to suit our temperament(s) to succeed in our relationships. In addition, we will examine how highly charged emotional environments (such as during upbringing or from broken previous relationships) can affect our relationship meter and make it more difficult to make it in relationships and in building strong bonds and connections within the family.

2
I Blame My Parents

Genetics, or your inherited genes and DNA, not only determine your physical looks such as your skin and eye color, but it also determine your core temperament which in turn determines your behavior in life and compatibility in relationships.

Each one of us is born with certain temperament traits that predispose us to interact with people and do things in a certain way. These temperaments are unique to us and they are what makes us do what we do, why we do it, and how we do it. Hence, core temperaments explain individual differences and is the foundation from which we build our values, shape our preferences and formulate our reactions and responses. It explains why some learn by watching, listening or by doing.

The original definition of temperaments was introduced in 1987 (Goldsmith et al). The commentator of the paper Robert McCall defined temperament as the following:

> *"Temperament consists of relatively consistent, basic dispositions inherent in the person that underlie and modulate the expression of activity, reactivity, emotionality, and sociability. Major elements of temperament are present early in life, and those items are likely to be strongly influenced by biological factors. As development proceeds, the expression of character increasingly becomes more influenced by experience and context."* (p. 524)

Based on the above definition we can understand that temperaments are one of personality components where it describes a relatively stable behavioural pattern that is observable from birth. Advances in molecular genetics and neuroscience and the employment of behavioural genetic techniques allowed psychologists to consider more seriously that individualized personalities disposition has biological roots. Since individuals display specific characteristic patterns of behaviour since birth, temperaments are considered biologically based and genetically determined. Therefore, temperaments may be considered "Core" personality that are formed before birth and way before we are influenced by others and cultural belief systems. These core temperaments are stable throughout our lifespan and they express themselves consistently through different situations and are the biological component of personality.

Now that we have talked about the core temperaments, let us move ahead to learn more about these temperament styles and how they affect our emotionality and the way we deal with emotions, which is the subject of this book.

Before we start talking about the core temperaments, I ought to point out these temperaments are descriptive and not prescriptive. They are neither good or bad and information presented here is to bring awareness on how you deal with your emotions based on your temperament type, which will in turn help you be a more emotionally competent individual. Being more emotionally competent will help you not only deal with your own emotions, but also will equip you with the tools and strategies to deal with others around you and to raise more competent children who will transfer this knowledge to their children for generations to come. Can you now see the domino effect of transforming your life today and how you can change the legacy you leave for future generations? Having this knowledge will not only make you successful in your relationships, but will also help you be successful in business and career. It will allow you to deal better with your coworkers and boss, it will tremendously reduce stress in your life, be happier, and more focused on your strengths rather than your weaknesses.

I guess by now you have figured out the answer to the title question in this chapter. But hold your horses, because even though 50% of your temperament is rooted in your genetics, you still have control over the rest 50%, which you will learn about in the following chapters.

3
Am I a Thinker or A Doer?

There are four distinct temperament styles that dictate our behaviour, needs, fear, emotional stress and compatibility in relationships. These are: the influencer, the supporter, the thinker, and the achiever. While there are aspects of each character in each of us, individuals typically exhibit one to two dominant styles that influence how they interact.

1- The Creative Influencer

You are an influencer if you love to help people and influence them. You are good with people and information and others love to be around you. People want your attention and want your attention if famous and they will follow your charisma. You are highly creative and artistic, and you like to be the centre of attention. Influencers are called dreamers and they are effective communicators. You are drawn to expressive outlets like writing, acting, or organizing games around friends. You value friendships and you enjoy life and like to have fun.

2- The Adaptive Supporter

As the name suggests, you are the supporter and helper in family and at work. You are flexible and adapt to situations easily. You are good with people and have interpersonal skills that helps you connect easily to others. Supporters are big on honesty and integrity and do not like being around others who do not display these trait qualities. Supporters are highly perceptive and can feel when others are not honest with them. You know you are a supporter when you find yourself in situations where you play the role of the peacekeeper and negotiator and you do not like arguments or illness amongst people close to you. You value harmony and disharmony affects you deeply and often you internalize it to avoid conflict. You value secure relationships and stable environments and that is why you are the most resistant to change unless you plan for it ahead of time.

3- **The Observer Thinker**

You are a thinker if you find yourself spending time thinking a lot about life and you like to examine issues in great detail. You take instructions well, organized, good with information, and you are a team player. You are good with math and numbers and you spend long hours on the computer. You are the detective. You like putting pieces of the puzzle together and come up with solutions to problems.

4- **The Achiever Doer**

You are an achiever if you value your independence and you have great need for self-expression. You are bold, productive, competitive, unemotional, and self-reliant. You rarely talk about your problems or emotions, instead you set goals and act independently. You are a born leader and you enjoy being recognized for your achievements. Achievers are persistent, and they think their way is the best way to doing things. They are your typical Type A personality in thinking and relating to others.

Did you figure out who you are and what is your core temperament? Do you have a primary and a secondary core temperament or you have a strong primary core temperament expressed behaviour? Now that you have figured that out let us move on to figure out how you deal with your emotions and what is your mental, emotional characteristics and your core emotional blueprint tendency.

4

Core Emotional Blueprint Tendencies

Each of the core temperaments is associated with certain traits and behaviours, which determines how individuals deal with emotions. It is important to recognize that whatever your core emotional blueprint is to understand how you deal with your emotions will affect people around you and take responsibility for your role in having harmonious or discord relationships in your life.

Are you ready for the next step?

Let's go…

1- The Creative Influencer

The influencer seeks pleasure, attention and gets bored easily. While you are sincere and cheerful, you are quick to become angry and prefer verbal expression of that anger. Once you have finished that expression, you move on and you don't hold grudges. You are enthusiastic and expressive. You are affectionate and like to express and demonstrate your emotions to others. Influencers get bored easily, hate to be alone, and fear rejection from others and being excluded. Since they like to be at the centre of attention and running the show, their fear of being excluded can make them to do things to gain others acceptance. Their way of dealing with fear is to ignore it and they mask that feeling with being more out there, being compulsive talkers, and restless. Fear of rejection and repression is their worst nightmare.

The fear of being alone can get the influencer first to surround himself/herself with the wrong kind of crowd, and second may not allow for establishing close and intimate relationships. Moreover, if the influencer lacks self-esteem he/she may indulge in destructive behaviours just to get attention, and many influencers may end up working in industries that will make it easy for them to do so.

If your core temperament characteristic is an influencer, then watch for the two emotions of anger and fear. I believe due to the nature of this temperament, anger is not something the influencer will have to worry about. The influence likes to have fun and enjoy life, and once the anger is blurted out verbally, they can get back to being the fun people they are. To learn how to deal with those two emotions go to chapters 7 and 9.

2- The Adaptive Supporter

Supporters tend to internalize emotions and only display them in private or with a trusted friend or colleague. They are the harmonizers, negotiators and peacekeepers in the family and at work. They avoid conflict at any cost and they do not express their emotions loudly or publicly. They can fall into moodiness and then into depression because they hate sharing thoughts with others. Supporters are that kind of people who suffer in silence while portraying a smiley façade. They are heart-centred, and their motivation is to help others.

I bet you million dollars you know many supporters around you whether it is the nurse at the clinic, the teacher at school, the administrative assistant at the office that supports your whole team, or sport coach. You will find a supporter around the corner if you looked carefully and you may be one yourself.

I can write books about this temperament and the nature of its core emotional blueprint. As a supporter, for most of my life I tried to keep my emotions in and when faced with emotional stress I retired to my little corner to keep peace and harmony. I developed the "pleaser syndrome" because I wanted everyone around me to be happy. I put my own happiness and emotions second to everyone else around me, which after years of imbalances turned into depression. It was hard for me to believe that I can get to that stage with me wearing that big smile on my face and having an optimistic outlook on life.

People thought I was the happiest person on earth, but what they did not know is that I was suffering alone on the inside but did not like to share my emotions with others so as not to make them unhappy. It was important for me to see others happy and putting a smile on their faces was more important than my own happiness. I grew up in an emotionally charged household and there was a lot of turmoil most of the time, therefore did not want to add to the cloud of misery hanging over our heads that could have rained tears at any moment. I know first hand how this temperament style can cause ill health if one is not armed with life skills to deal with these types of emotions. Therefore, it is very critical for the supporters to learn how to be happy on the inside and not just make others happy. If sadness is one of the negative emotions that is engrained in your core emotional blueprint, then go to chapter 8 where you will find tools to help you deal with your sadness and grief.

3- The Observer Thinker

The observer is a loner and enjoys the company of their own thoughts. They are shy and take time to warm up to others, which at times you maybe perceived as being unsocial. The thinkers do not show their emotions on the outside, however, on the inside they can internalize their feelings with tears and depression rather than with rage. Unlike the influencers who forgive and forget, thinkers can hold a grudge against people who hurt them, they may not easily forgive them and let them back into their lives.

Thinkers are perfectionists by nature and because of that they worry about life. They worry about the past and they project it to the future. Hence, thinkers need to watch for that emotion and be aware this is one of their temperament characteristics that may explain the way they feel rather than beating themselves up worrying about things. To learn how to deal with worry, go to chapter 9.

4- The Achiever Doer

The last temperament to talk about is the Achiever or Doer type. Achievers rise to the occasion when they are challenged, and they expect rewards for winning. They are not sensitive to emotions and they consider it a weakness. They are not sympathetic to display of emotions such as crying and tears. They are aggressive rather than assertive and are quick to fire up anger. They are moody, and their impatience can quickly turn into anger and then rage. The above qualities make Doers excellent leaders. They strive to win and to be successful because they are persistent and inflexible. When it comes to the job, all they care about is knowing the job is going to be done rather than learning the facts or how it will be done. To the Doer time is money so do not waste any time. These are your typical Type A personality. They live in tension and mostly suffer from adrenal fatigue because the overdrive life that they live.

Are you or someone around you exhibiting this emotional tendency? How does expressing emotions in such a manner affect your relationships with others around you? If you identify with the emotion of anger and blurting out verbal words that hurt others during bouts of anger, then tools presented in chapter 10 will help you break up with anger once and for all.

Going back to Malcolm's story. Malcolm had the Doer temperament, which meant he was more prone to being angry if he didn't know how to handle his temper. His energy was out of balance and due to his negative upbringing experiences, he harbored a lot of anger and resentment that characterized his behaviour. His motto was "*my way or the highway*" and "*dare you stand in my way, I'll crush you.*" He alienated his family, friends, and coworkers. He reached a point where he could not work with anyone and isolated himself from others where his only companion was his computer.

The thing about Malcolm is that he did not want to change his behaviour, nor admit he had an issue that needed his attention. Living with anger will end up burning the person who is harboring it and it consumes all his energy that in the end he will run out of fuel to feed his life. This is exactly what happened to Malcolm, which was unfortunate. Had he acknowledged that he had a problem, and accepted help offered to him over the years, he would have been able to work on his healing, would have amazing relationships in his life, left a legacy other than hate and anger, and he would have been successful in life.

It is sad to see many people going through life not knowing how to deal with their negative emotions and when they start their own family they pass on these emotions to their children unless the other parent is strong enough to change this family culture and bring more balance and harmony to the household. That is exactly why I am writing this book. I want to help you, the reader, to learn more about your temperament and the type of emotion that you are more disposed to heal the child within before you start a family and pass on those negative emotions to them.

This type of behaviour of losing anger quickly is not new to me. I grew up in a family culture that is characterized by quick anger. My father and uncles expressed their emotions through screaming, yelling, and spilling out their beans at the first person they encounter when they get mad.

My dad and uncles are the nicest people you can ever meet, however, that was their nature and how they dealt with things when they got angry. This kind of behaviour makes it hard for people around them deal with them when they are on top of the anger wave. Despite them being kind and compassionate, loosing

Core Emotional Blueprint Tendencies

their temper easily disrupts peace in the family and all communication shuts down because other family members cannot tame the fire flames that just flared up in their faces. This in turn, will create another negative emotion, which is fear. I remember when my dad used to lose his temper, I was paralyzed with fear. Now let us be clear here, such behaviour can affect people differently depending on their temperament. For example, such behaviour affected me more than my sibling due to my nature and my core temperament of being a harmonizer.

The issue with any negative behaviour is that it will be carried on to future generations if no one does anything about it. Parents model for their children what type of behaviour to choose and demonstrate. If a parent is quick to be angry and starts yelling and screaming, then what is it that he/she is modeling for the child? What are they teaching their children about communication style? And how would that child then raise his/her own children. Yes, core temperament determines your nature, but let us not forget that is only half of your personality and remember that you have a choice in how you express a certain behaviour and modify the environment to suit your character.

Now that we know more about the effects of biology and genetics that shapes 50% of our personality and how we behave, let us move on to the other 50% that shapes the rest of our behaviour and that is "the environment". Or is it really the case? Let us learn more about emerging research about the role of genetics and epigenetics in shaping our temperament and their role in our behaviour.

5
Epigenetic Factors

I have mentioned earlier our genetics is responsible for half of our traits and behaviour and the other half is influenced by the environment. The question that begs itself at this point is when does the environment shape our experiences? Is it something that affects us before birth or after birth? To answer this question, we need to have a look at emerging research in the area of human behaviour.

New research has shown not all temperament traits are stable early in life due to the presence of other factors that may control or inhibit the more reactive aspects of temperaments and will emerge only later in infancy. These control factors may change the expression and stability of the more reactive traits and characteristics (Rothbart, 2011). Having said that, traits become more consistent with age showing substantial stability in the preschool years (Roberts & DelVecchio, 2000).

Biology determines our traits in the beginning and even before a child is born. If you come to think about it, the first environment the child is exposed to is the mother's womb and, therefore, it makes sense to think that environmental factors affect us as soon as we are conceived. If that environment was healthy and robust, then the child is set with a great start. Research has shown that before a child's birth, the uterus environment has already influenced the expression of genes (Huizink 2012) and experiences continue to shape genetic expression after birth (Champagne & Mashoodh, 2009, Saudino & Wang, 2012).

Based on the above, one can argue that environmental factors affect temperaments before the child is born, which means both biological and environmental factors shape our traits and dispositions early on in life. Taken all together, we can conclude that the foundation of our temperament is genetically laid and then life experiences adds another layer to our biological blueprint to form the whole person. This information is critical to our understanding of the importance of the emotional environment the mother lives in during her pregnancy. Dr. Thomas Verny, who is the founder of the Association for Prenatal and Perinatal Psychology and Health (APPPAH) and Journal of Prenatal and Perinatal Psychology and Health, says that *"Everything the pregnant mother feels, and thinks is communicated through neurohormones to her unborn child, just as surely as are alcohol and nicotine"* confirming the notion that temperaments are influenced by the environment before the child is born.

Studying Chinese Medicine over the past ten years opened my mind to the effect of environmental factors such as food, lifestyle, and emotions on our well-being. In Chinese philosophy, which is based on the free flow of energy in the body, the environment plays a pivotal role in wellbeing. Being in tune with nature, eating according to the season, and keeping emotions in check are some of the basic tenants of Chinese Medicine. Living a life that is not in alignment with the above can cause disharmony and ill health.

Emotions can cause energy (Qi) stagnation in the body if they are not kept in check and the home and family life plays a great role in the development of child's health.

What we are talking about here is not only physical abusive environments, but also the emotional abuse and the unintended emotional energy the child is raised in. Emotions will cause us stress and it is this long-term unresolved stress that leads to weakness of energy of ill health. Stress is more dangerous to children due to their reliance on their essence energy to help them grow. Therefore, if the mother is living in stressful conditions and is dealing with extreme emotions, then her unborn child is also affected by that.

According to Chinese Medicine, each emotion is associated with one organ and it affects the free flow of energy in that organ. For example, anger affects the liver, fear affects the kidneys, while sadness and grief affect the lungs. If the mother is feeling these emotions, then stress hormones are produced in her body which can penetrate the placenta and get to the unborn child. Accordingly, the child will be stressed and dealing with the same emotion the mother is exposed to. This is why it is critical for parents to realize how negative emotions affect their unborn baby and start preparing for the birth of the child by reducing any negative emotions in their environment and reduce their impact on their child.

Do you notice how sometimes some children are born anxious and nervous and keep crying for no apparent reason? If you look back at the mother's pregnancy you will probably see the mother was living in stress, either at work or at home, which in turn affected the baby. To the contrary, another mother who spent her pregnancy in a calm, quiet home listening to music and nurturing herself and the baby, her newborn baby will be calm and quiet. Don't take my word for it, just look around and inspect this issue for yourself.

Environmental factors are also determined by the culture we grow up in and that is an important factor in determining our personality and what shapes our preferences in life. Growing up in a conservative culture in the Middle East, I can attest to the role of the environment in shaping our personalities and the detrimental effects it has on our choices in life if we allow the culture to take over our lives.

In the following chapters, I'll be talking about the four emotional blueprint tendencies I mentioned previously and how to deal with such negative emotions. Despite being a supporter and being more prone to sadness, the environment I grew up in shaped my personality where I harbored the rest of the emotional blueprints, and that is why you'll find my story woven into each of the following chapters in the hope my reader to learn more about the effects of the environment on our behaviour. Having this awareness at the forefront of our minds will shift our lives and the way we allow environmental factors to affect our behaviour, our careers, our relationships, and the way we deal with life.

6
Genetics, Epigenetics, and Energetics

In my previous book "Shift to Shine: Bridging Science and Intuition", I introduced the concept of energetic genes (you can purchase the e-book from www.rajamishal.com and from Amazon worldwide).

In Shift to Shine I coined the term "Psychological Energetic Values Genes, PEVs" referring to those energetic genes that are stored in our psyche (has nothing to do with psychology). In the same way, we inherited our genes and their characteristics at the physical level, we inherited our Psychological Energetic Values genes and their characteristics at the energetic level. These genes were transferred to us through our parents and our culture, and were encoded into our psyche.

We were conditioned with those PEVs in our early years of life and through our adulthood in a way that was dependent on our household and our culture. PEVs dictate who we are at the core of our human being and at the energetic level of our psychological behaviour.

In our genome, some genes are present in clusters or in a gene family encode similar characteristics and share a general function. Likewise, at the energetic level, PEV genes are present in clusters that produce certain values, which will result in our predisposition to certain traits and characteristics and usually when one of those energetic genes is present, its sisters or cousins' energetic genes accompany it because it is rare we are only affected by one negative emotion.

As stated above, the energetic gene cluster contains all kind of values that when present in the right dose will produce the best characteristics in an individual. However, as with anything, an over-expression or under-expression of these values will tip the balance and will cause disharmony and blockages in the flow of energy. Moreover, more than one energetic gene may be expressed at the same time. For example, if we express the fear energetic gene, the anger or worry energetic gene is activated at the same time.

This is exactly what happened with me when I had to deal with more than one emotion at a time, even though I was more predisposed to one emotion and that is sadness. Therefore, when dealing with those energetic genes it may take longer to peel all these layers of energetic expression before we are able to shift them energetically and move to a more positive higher vibration. Hence, it is critical for us to learn how to deal with the expression of these negative emotions and not only with our own emotional blueprint.

First, we learn our core temperament, our values, needs, fears, and what motivates us and then we learn how to deal with the energetic genes and emotions to be able to create a healthy and balanced families. It is of utmost priority to parent the child within and care for it before we start our own families to build stronger generations and create healthy relationships that will make us and everyone around us happy.

So, let us move on to learn how to deal with those emotional blueprints tendencies and energetic genes.

7
The Fear of Losing the Circus

The Influencer's emotional blueprint tendency is fear. This energetic gene may be expressed in several ways. For example, influencers may be afraid of believing in themselves. They may have self-doubt about their work and their creativity or originality. Fear of being liked by others, fear of being not the centre of attention, fear of not being in the spot light, and fear of not being taken seriously by others.

A friend of mine who lives overseas has the typical characteristics of an Influencer. He is an amazing artist who performs on stage and in front of the camera in short films. He is loved by everyone, he is always at your service, and on top of that he is very humorous. His fear of being rejected by others made him a pleaser. He will do anything to please people around him and eventually, he became a clown in his own circus until he learned how to deal with his own fear, rejection. That is when he used his inherited characteristics and traits to influence people without him making a fool of himself. Once he focused on his strengths and learned how to value himself, he attracted the right kind of crowd into his life where he formed a team of great talented young actors and actresses. He directed famous theatrical plays, which won him awards and made him one of the few famous icons in the theatre world overseas.

Let me tell you about my own story with fear. Fear has been part of my life since I can remember. Fear of upsetting my father and getting him angry, fear of disappointing my parents if I did not get high grades at school, fear of what people around me think about me, fear of crossing a red light, fear of seeing a policeman, fear of standing up for myself, fear of voicing my opinion, fear of doing what is right for me, fear of leaving dysfunctional marriages, fear of not finding a job and hence the fear of not being able to have a working visa to stay in the country, fear of facing certain cultural and religious dogmas, and so on…you get the idea. Fear energy was surrounding me wherever I went, and it became ingrained in my psyche to the extent it totally crippled me. My decisions were based on and stemmed from fear.

Fear is one of the energetic genes I inherited from my family, reinforced by the culture I was brought up in at that time. The dynamics in my family was slightly different to many of the families I grew up with. The energetic charge in my household was negative most of the time. The energy of fear, anger, sadness and anxiety ruled our household. The way I dealt with this negativity was by spending every waking minute of my life focusing on my studies.

Growing up the fear energy continued to pile up, becoming darker and denser in my energy field until I physically collapsed and was no longer able to function. I was a walking fear energetic-being among other negative energies. I attracted to my personal life, despite a huge success at the professional level, negative energies.

Fear is that we are in danger and at times, it has nothing to do with the reality of the situation. It is what we build in our mind and our own perception of a situation. Some of those fears are legitimate while others are not. I believe one of those fears imposed on us "the culture fear". The fear of doing something that is culturally unacceptable is the worst kind of fear anyone can face for it is the hardest to break away from, and it will hold us prisoner in our own mind.

It took me eighteen years to break away from an abusive husband, even though I was living in Canada in a culture that allows women to leave their violent husbands in a country that gives rights to females to take the steps to end a relationship. Nevertheless, in my mind that was something totally unacceptable because in my culture this is shunned, especially as it was my second marriage. That kind of fear kept me hostage in a dysfunctional marriage for the fear of judgement and consequently for the devastating effects on my children. It took me a long time to muster the courage to leave the marriage and break away from the cultural dogma around such an issue. However, I had to pay a high price for standing up for myself and my children at the personal, professional, financial and cultural levels.

The fear of our actions being judged by the culture has nothing to do with a certain ethnic group or for that matter, being a male or female.

Over the years, I met so many men and women who could not take action because of cultural belief systems that held them back. For example, many men and women stayed in dysfunctional marriages either because of their children, or for the fear of being an outcast in their community.

If you think this only happens in the migrant or new comer to the society, think twice. When I finally mustered the courage to leave my second husband I noticed many of the people I knew stayed away from me, and I was not invited or welcomed at my friends' gatherings – and this behaviour came from both my immigrant and Canadian friends. To my amazement, I knew the same was true in the Canadian born and raised community, which indicates this issue is a trans-cultural issue.

I believe much of the negative and undesirable results I expressed due to my own fear energy also had to do with my personality and my temperament. Adaptive supporters are more sensitive than others because their life purpose is to help others, which in turn will affect how they respond to certain energies in their environment. You can liken this to how the application of heat to different elements, for example wood or metal, will produce different results based on the specific inherent properties of that element.

Knowing what I know today about myself and my temperament there was no other way I would have been able to respond to negative emotions and energetic genes other than the way I did. Being born an empath, sensitive to peoples' emotions, wanting to help others, believing unconditional love is the way to go made me more **susceptible** to these negative energies and take it all in, rather than clearing them out. It would have been nice if I had known all about temperaments, energy and the energy field at that time, or yet even better if I had a mentor or someone in my life to point me in the right direction; nevertheless, that was not the case.

I cannot dwell on it at this point, and in fact the way I look at it now is that I had to go through all of those fear energetic-challenges in order for me to be the person I am today. These experiences shaped my life and put me on this path in order to help others, and bring awareness to their conscious mind in the hope of minimizing the challenges they go through to build robust relationships that will make them happy. My journey was not easy, but that does not mean you have to go through these challenges in order for you to learn what I have over the years. I learned these lessons in order for me to pass them onto you, and help you pass these tests easily if you encounter them in your life or if you chose them as part of your earthly journey.

In my case, I had to deal with the fear energy even though my emotional blueprint tendency is sadness. However, the environment adapted the expression of my other energetic genes and allowed for them to be highly expressed along with sadness. Influencers have it in them to be the centre of attention and they are the ones who want to be running the circus of life. They gravitate towards professions in which they are the centre of attention and famous, such as singers, writers, speakers, politicians and artists. These professions are highly stressful and add more pressure on influencers to be more creative and to provide exceptional performances, which feeds into the feeling of influencing others. That is why we tend to see some Influencers in the media industry use alcohol and drugs to deal with the enormous amount of pressure imposed on them in order to please their audience.

Fear energy is very dense and heavy and the way it affects us physiologically is by increasing our heart rate, decreasing appetite, having shortness of breath, and anxiety. Fear energy is stored in the kidneys and adrenals, according to Chinese Medicine, and the adrenals are responsible for the fight or flight response when we are faced with danger. You can start today shifting the fear energy by practicing one of the oldest healing modalities in Chinese Medicine, Qigong (pronounced chee gong), to help you strengthen your Kidneys' energy to purge fear.

The following simple Qigong exercises can be practiced anywhere and anytime during the day, for any length of time. You could start with two minutes and increase the amount of time you spend doing the exercise. As with any Qigong internal healing exercise, you need to start with the intention. So, your intention for these exercises will be to increase your Kidney energy and purge fear.

1) *Tapping and Rubbing the Kidneys*

    This exercise can be performed either standing or sitting, or even lying on your tummy if you want to. I recommend you start your day with a few minutes of tapping the kidneys, which will not only help you strengthen their energy – and in turn will help get rid of fear - but it will definitely give you a great energy boost and will stimulate your adrenals to deal with the stressors that are coming your way. Tapping the kidneys will increase the secretions of the adrenal glands, will increase the blood flow to the kidneys enhancing their energy, help dissolve crystals before they form kidney stones, and will help boost your immune system.

    a. From a standing or sitting position raise your hands behind your back, the kidney is at the bottom of the rib cage.
    b. Start tapping the kidneys gently with the back of your hand or with your fists. Please do not tap hard in this area as you do not want to cause any damage to the kidneys and because you may be sensitive in this area.

    c. Tap both kidneys at the same time for several minutes. You will feel energized and invigorated in only few minutes of doing so.

    d. When you are done tapping start rubbing the kidneys using a flat palm by going up and down until you feel warmth in the area. Again, this may take one to two minutes.

2) <u>*Taking in the Blue Light Meditation*</u>

    a- Begin in a standing, sitting, or lying position

    b- Relax the whole body and release any wondering thoughts

    c- Imagine a blue energy in front of you. While inhaling, draw the blue light energy through the nose and into the Kidneys.

    d- As you exhale through the mouth, the dark turbid energy leaves the Kidneys; however, the bright blue color stays in the lungs stimulating and vitalizing them.

    e- Repeat for 5 breaths

    f- Next, breathe in blue color through the nose filling the entire mouth.

g- Exhale through the nose and send this blue light energy slowly down to the Kidneys.
h- Repeat 6 to 12 breaths.
i- Close the exercise by visualizing the energy in your Kidneys melting down into your belly on your final exhale.

3) *Affirmations*

In addition to strengthening the Kidney's Qi (energy), we can do daily positive affirmations that will help the conscious mind in attaining our goal of removing negative fear energy, which keeps us stuck in unhealthy situations. You can choose affirmations you connect with, makes you feel good about saying them and invokes a positive emotional response. The affirmations must be stated in the present tense, be short, and focused on the negative fear energy that is holding you back in the current situation. Examples of these affirmations are:

- All is well in my world and I know that all is taken care of
- I am willing to release fear and be open for receiving love

- I trust in Divine order and know I am looked after at all times
- I let go of controlling the current situation and surrender to what is
- I trust that I am divinely protected
- I release all negative fear and doubt

8

A Smiley Face and a Sad Heart

The adaptive supporters' core emotional blueprint tendency is sadness, and as discussed in previous chapters other negative emotions can also be expressed along with sadness. Due to the nature of the supporters they are also more prone to express other energetic genes values such as worry and fear. The sadness emotion is not limited to this temperament since it is one of the vital and basic emotions that makes us human.

Based on our temperament and the environment we grow up in, this emotion may be more predominant in some than in others but if you have the adaptive supporter temperament, then due to your nature you may find yourself keeping your emotions in and not sharing them with others for the sake of making others around you happy. That is not to say you are not a happy person, to the contrary, you are an optimistic and happy person. However, you put others' happiness ahead of yours, which makes you compromise your own happiness and be a supporter martyr until you learn how to value, love, and put yourself first and others second.

In my years of practice, I saw the sadness energetic gene repeatedly. There is so much sadness going around that no wonder one of the highest rates of death is from lung and colon cancer.

If we are to live only once, why are we living our lives in sadness? How come we do not wake up every day with the intention to be happy no matter what life throws at us? Being happy is your birthright and is a state of being. You must claim it back if you have lost it. Life is too short to be lived in sadness, willow and sorrow. Dwelling and sweating the little things in life is not conducive to our wellbeing and will always keep us in a lower energetic vibration, which will attract more negativity into our lives. Yes, there are times where we are sad, and we grieve the loss of a loved one or a close relationship in our lives, however, that does not mean you have to stay in that energy.

According to Traditional Chinese Medicine, the psycho-emotional aspects of grief, sadness, integrity, and attachment are related to the lungs. Should someone continue to harbor this energy in their psyche, they will end up with all kinds of physical ailments such as asthma, allergies, skin issues, and sinusitis. Being out of balance for a long time with other emotions such as fear, worry, or anger will also affect the flow of energy in the lungs and will cause disharmony in the long term, therefore, it is critical to stay on top of our emotions and deal with them as soon as they surface in order to be happy. How do you expect to make others happy when you are not happy on the inside? What supporters tend to forget is that happiness comes from within and not from pleasing others, and that it is okay to be happy and share our emotions with others when we feel sad and down. Suppressing our emotions for a long time will lead us to feel helpless and despair, which will lead into anxiety, depression and other illnesses.

In my upcoming book "Hope Rises: The Power of Taking Action", I talk about depression and mental illness and how to get out of it using a holistic approach. In the meantime, here are some strategies to help you release sadness and be happy again in your relationships.

The following exercise and meditation are one of my favorite exercises to release the emotion of grief and sadness and to strengthen the Lungs energy. The first exercise uses healing sounds to purge any deep-seated emotions, while the second one is a meditation that uses the color of the Lungs organ in Traditional Chinese Medicine to strengthen the Lungs energy.

1) <u>Healing sounds</u>

   Healing sounds are one of my favorite exercises to deal with any disharmony in the organs and to release negative emotions. A word of caution before you start this exercise though, healing sounds are very powerful, and you may feel agitated when you initially do this exercise so be patient and continue doing it, unless you really feel it is affecting you negatively. If that is the case, stop doing the exercise for few days, then try again and see how you feel. Another word of caution is that pregnant women should not perform this exercise, if you are sick, or if you have any broken bones in the body.

   There are two healing sounds for the lung that resonate with the lungs energy, therefore, choose the one that feels better for you.

a- Begin by standing, sitting upright in a chair, or lying in bed.
b- Place both palms flat on the sides of the chest.
c- Focus the mind's intention on the Lung area.
d- Perform the Lung Massage while inhaling slowly (circulate the hands up and down in a circular motion).
e- Exhale and sound the word "Sssssss", or "Shhhhhhh" while rubbing the chest with both palms.
f- Repeat the exercise for 6 to 12 breaths. Start with 3 breaths and increase gradually over time if you cannot do 6 to 12 breaths.

2) *Taking in the White Light Meditation*

This is a meditation that can be used to strengthen the Lungs energy. The inherent properties of the color white have a vibrational quality that strengthens the Lungs and the Large Intestine.

j- Begin in a standing, sitting, or lying position.

k- Relax the whole body and release any wondering thoughts.
l- Imagine a white energy in front of you. While inhaling, draw the white light energy through the nose and into the Lungs.
m- As you exhale through the mouth, the dark turbid energy leaves the Lungs; however, the bright white color stays in the lungs stimulating and vitalizing them.
n- Repeat for 5 breaths
o- Next, breathe in white color through the nose filling the entire mouth.
p- Exhale through the nose and send this white light energy slowly down to the Lungs.
q- Repeat 9 to 18 breaths.
r- Close the exercise by visualizing the energy in your Lungs melting down into your belly on your final exhale.

The above exercises will not only help release deep seated emotions but will increase your energy, vitalizes you, and will help keep your immune system strong. Over time, you may feel that allergies will be lessened, and you may catch a cold less often.

9
Worry Kills Intimacy

One of the emotional blueprints of the observant thinker is worry. Thinkers worry because they want to be perfectionists, which is one of their temperaments. They worry about things that happened in the past and they project that worry into the future. Thinkers must be aware of this emotional blueprint, so they can control their worry. One thought of worry is fine, but having many thoughts of worry that work in concert with each other will manifest themselves into anxiety that may affect their personal life and their performance at work.

When worry is brought into a relationship, it will quickly diminish its success rate to zero as it is one of the hardest energies to deal with for the thinker's partner, who will not understand the basis of this temperament and its behaviour. Worry robs the thinker from living in the moment and being present with others, and in turn will result in loss of joy and feeling intimacy in a relationship, which is one of the thinker's core values. The thinker parent will also tend to be perceived by other family members as controlling, creating more rebelliousness in the family and especially in children who try to escape as far as they can from the controlling parent. At work, the thinker's worry can be channeled in a positive way to keep projects on time, tasks accomplished, and projects seen into completion.

The emotional energy charge of worry was part of growing up in the Middle East. For instance, one of the thoughts always on foreigners' minds who were born and raised in Kuwait was the worry of staying in the country. Foreigners needed a working visa to stay in Kuwait and a loss of job meant the loss of their working visa and, hence, the departure from the country. It would not be such a problem if individuals moved there on a contract, knowing at the end of the contract they had to leave the country. Nonetheless, for us individuals who were born and raised in Kuwait and never visited their country of origin it was a tragic disaster.

This type of worry goes against the cultural core belief system I grew up with, in which God always takes care of us and that jobs and money are always in his hands. The reality is that people still worried about their job and income at the unconscious level.

The emotional energy of worry is stored in the spleen (and pancreas) according to Chinese Medicine. In the philosophy of Chinese Medicine, the spleen plays a huge role in digestion. Worry and pensiveness will block the flow of its energy and will interfere with its function and ability to absorb nutrients from the food we eat. Hence, long hours of mental work and worry will damage the spleen's energy and causes symptoms such as nausea, loose stool, fatigue, heaviness, poor appetite among other symptoms. No wonder I had a lot of digestive issues growing up!

Trust is one of the higher vibrational energies that can combat worry. Having trust in a higher power and believing things will always fall in place at the right time is the key to releasing worry energy. Again, according to the law of attraction, if you focus your energy on worry then all you are going to attract into your life is worry. Easier said than done. True. However, like everything we have been talking about so far, it is your choice. You make that choice to trust and let go of wanting to control everything around you and things will happen at the right time when they are meant to be.

As worry is a thought that needs to be watched by the conscious mind, which will eventually change the pattern in the unconscious mind, it will be very helpful to work with positive affirmations for a period of thirty days until the unconscious mind believe this new pattern. Here is how you can do it:
Write the following affirmations on sticky notes and put them everywhere around you. Stick the notes to the bathroom mirror so it will be the very first thing you see in the morning, stick it on your fridge, on the door, on your way out of the house, in the car, in your office etc... After a while, change the location of the sticky notes so you can pay attention to them again. You can say whatever you want that is positive, will bring you joy, and calm your mind from your worries. For instance, you can say:

a. I am letting go of my worries
b. All is well
c. All my needs are met

d. I am looked after all the time
e. I trust in a divine order
f. My mind is relaxed and thinking clearly
g. I am at peace
h. Letting go of my worries help me stay calm and relaxed

Another strategy to deal with worry is to practice some relaxation techniques that will not only help calm the mind, but also help deal with the physical symptoms of worry and muscle tension. Since it is hard to quiet the mind chatter when we are worried and anxious, I like the following muscle relaxation technique "Progressive Muscle Relaxation" or PMR since it keeps the mind engaged and focused on relaxing each part of the body. When I started using this technique, I recorded the exercise and listened to it every night before going to sleep. To my busy mind it was the perfect technique to start with; it was easy to follow and put me in touch with my own physical body where it allowed me to feel what tension felt like in my body. Once you have practiced this technique for a period of a month or two, you may be able to find yourself move to other forms of mindfulness that will quiet your thoughts through sitting meditation.

This relaxation technique involves tensing and relaxing all the various muscle groups in the body in a specific sequence. During stressful times, we tend to worry more and be more anxious or fearful, which will lead us to store tension in our muscles and by consciously tightening the muscles and releasing them beyond their normal tension we can suddenly relax them. Practice this relaxation technique for 20–30 minutes daily before going to bed or before you get out of bed in the morning.

There are many ways of practicing the muscle group relaxation, however, I am going to show you the way I initially learned where you start at the feet and going all the way up to the head, so here you go:

Tighten each muscle for few seconds and then release the tension before moving to the next group of muscles. Go through the whole cycle once and repeat it one or two more times until you feel completely relaxed.

1) Curl your toes and tighten them as much as you can. Hold this position for few seconds and then release. Pay attention to the sensations in the muscles as you contract and release the tension.
2) Tighten shin and calf muscles. Hold, and then release.
3) Tense your inner thighs as hard as you can. Release and feel the legs relaxed.
4) Tighten the buttocks and the hip area pushing down into the bed or the chair you are sitting on. Release the tension.
5) Contract all the muscles in the abdomen and stomach area. Hold, and then release the contraction.
6) Hunch your shoulders up as high as you can. Hold, and then drop them down and relax. Feel the heaviness in the muscles as they relax. This is where a lot of people hold their tension in.
7) Gently arch your back as you take a deep breath. Hold, then relax.
8) Tense the whole arms. Hold, and then release the tension and feel the whole arms relaxed.

9) Make a fist with both of your hands and clench tightly. Hold the tightness and then release.
10) Tilt the head back as far as you can until it presses against the bottom of your neck. Hold and then release.
11) Tilt the head to one side so it reaches the shoulder. Hold, and then release. Repeat on the other side of the shoulder.
12) Bring the head forward and roll it clockwise in a complete circle then roll it once counter clockwise
13) Clench your jaw, hold, and then release. This is one area where most people feel their tension. Repeat several times if it feels good for you.
14) Tighten up the muscles in the entire face, hold and then release.
15) Close your eyes tightly and smile stretching the mouth as wide open as you can. Hold, and then release.
16) Raise your eyebrows up and high as you can to feel the tension in the forehead. Hold, and then drop the eyebrows and become smooth.
17) Repeat steps 1 – 16 one or two more times.

10
It is My Way or The Highway

Moving on now to talk about the last temperament and that is the Achiever Doer. The emotional blueprint for the Doer is anger. Because the Doers are driven leaders, highly competitive, fearless, independent, demanding, and risk-takers they get annoyed easily with others around them if their efforts are blocked or if they are challenged for control. Doers care only about results and getting things done, which make them insensitive to others' emotions or needs and they can come across as bullies.

Doers are visionaries and leaders but at the same time they are not sensitive to emotions and can erupt in anger quickly. Hence, it is important for Doers to learn strategies to control their anger in order to be effective and successful leaders at work and at home.

If we go back to Malcolm, we can clearly see that he is a Doer. In his relationship with his wife and children, he controlled every aspect of their lives. He would get upset and angry for the slightest reason and it would take him ages to calm down and back to talking to any of them. He always thought he was right and others were wrong and never ever admitted wrong doing. His family members had to live according to what he thought was right and he used to tell them *"my way or the highway. Dare you ever challenge my authority. I will crush you."* He bullied them by screaming, yelling, hitting, withdrawing emotionally, and controlling the household financially.

Malcolm was a victim of his own temperament that got the better of him. To add to this type of temperament, Malcolm was raised in a household where love was conditional, he was treated differently to his siblings, and he was controlled by his parents. Both of his parents were Doers, and each of them wanted to control the other parent and the rest of the family. With so much control in the family, Malcolm grew up learning that the only way to deal with others is through control, this was engrained in his energy and traits.

When Malcolm got married and started a family, he continued to be controlling and things worked for him for a long time, until the environment he lived in changed and he was no longer in control, which resulted in making him angry. Malcolm expressed his anger aggressively, eventually leading his wife and children to leave as they were fearful for their lives. Doers are usually aggressive when it comes to achieving their goals and having their needs met, but when it gets out of hand it turns into violence through bullying and abuse. We have many great leaders and visionaries that are Doers, however, if these Doers did not grow up in healthy environments then they tend to be more aggressive and they alienate everyone around them and tend to live their lives lonely even if they were in a relationship.

I was married to a Doer, and it was the worst combination ever in a relationship. I know so many supporters who were married to Doers and had to go through hardship in their relationships. The devastating effects of living with an abusive Doer is unbearable. What gives a human being the right to emotionally, mentally, and physically abuse someone else is beyond my comprehension.

Bullying others and coercing them into doing what someone wants is totally unacceptable, should not be tolerated, and must be banned completely in all cultures and societies. It is something that needs to be talked about and taught at school early in the education process. Both men and women need to be taught how to communicate their needs with respect and be sensitive to others needs.

Since Supporters like to support others and be of service they are usually taken advantage of in a relationship and can be abused by a bully Doer. Until Supporters stand up for themselves and draw the line and set limits for what is acceptable and what is not, the Doer will continue to control and unleash his anger on the Supporter. This can take any form of abuse from verbal, physical, emotional, mental, or financial. I truly believe that emotional abuse and neglect is by far worse than physical abuse and it takes a long time to heal from its wounds. The scars and bruises physical abuse leave on the body disappear within days and at the most weeks. The hidden scars of emotional abuse take not months but years to heal, and in so many cases are never healed. Let us not forget that emotional abuse did not come alone, it brought with it low self-esteem and self-worth and the "I am not good enough" energy. Add to the mix the fear factor and now you have a concoction of a tragedy soup in the making.

In my experience, the Doer and the Supporter temperaments combination are not compatible in relationships unless the Doer learns emotional sensitivity and the Supporter learns to draw limits and I had to learn this the hard way.

According to Chinese Medicine, anger affects the liver and over time, if this energy is not released or kept in check, it will affect the heart energy as the liver is the mother of the heart. Anger affects the heart indirectly and causes symptoms such as palpitations, shortness of breath, and cold limbs, among other symptoms. As you can see, one emotional energy not only affects the organ it is stored in, but eventually will affect the rest of the organs in the body, which will complicate things even further. Therefore, it is always best to deal with the negative energy as soon as we identify it and release it from our psyche before it starts to affect our lives and our relationships.

One of the simplest exercises that I learned during my Qigong studies to release anger is beating the pillow, so here it is:

Beating the Pillow Exercise

This is one of my favorite physical exercises to get rid of anger, especially if it has been bottled up for a long period of time. For this exercise, you are going to need a baseball bat and a pillow.

a. Find yourself a quiet place where you can spend time alone without any interruptions. You can choose a time where you are alone at home if you do not want others to know what you are doing, or you can tell the rest of the family that you are working on releasing your anger and there is no need for them to worry about you.
b. Take a deep breath in and then hit the pillow with your baseball bat as you breathe out.
c. As you breathe out make the sound "ha". Repeat several times for a period of 15 minutes

d. When you are done. Put away the pillow and the bat. **Never use this pillow to sleep on**.

Another favorite exercise of mine is internal organ massage. This simple, yet highly effective, exercise aids in the movement of energy for internal organs. It can be used for any of the organs, but I am going to use it in the next section as an exercise to aid in the regulation of liver's energy which in turn will help with regulating the emotion of the Liver which is anger.

Liver Qi (Energy) Massage

a) Begin by standing, sitting upright in a chair, or lying in bed.
b) Take three deep breaths inhaling in through the nose and exhaling out through the mouth.
c) Place your hands on the Liver (the liver situated on the right-hand side of the body underneath the rib cage). Focus your mind's intention on the Liver organ allowing the energy within the Liver area to flow and circulate with the movement of the hands.

d) Massage in twelve circular rotations to the left in a clockwise direction. The hands can either lightly touch the skin or be slightly off the skin up to several inches away from the body.
e) Imagine a bright green light energy in front of you. While inhaling, draw the bright green light through the nose and into the Liver.
f) As you exhale through the mouth, the dark turbid energy leaves the Liver; however, the bright green color stays in the Liver stimulating and vitalizing it.
g) Massage in twelve circular rotations in the opposite direction.
h) Repeat Liver Qi massage 8-12 times.

When I embarked on this new part of the journey, little did I know that I did so to heal myself before healing others. All the Qigong education I did over the years was to heal those parts in me that were broken and no one else could fix for me. I had to be the healer of my own wounds and it definitely took a lot of time, effort, patience and perseverance. No healing can occur without these factors and individuals should have the will power to take charge of their life in order to get rid of negative experiences and memories once and for all. No physician or an outside force can do that for you. Only you can heal you. If you want to be a better person, a better husband, a better wife, a better friend, a better family member, a better co-worker, a better parent, or a better version of you, you must start today healing those wounds you either inherited or acquired because of the environment you lived in.

It is critical for us to understand our core temperaments, strengths, weaknesses and our emotional blueprint tendencies. Once we understand what motivates us and what our needs and fears are, we can really understand who we are at the core of our being. This awareness will initiate our healing, it will allow us to parent the child within before we even think about starting a family. We may be wounded and broken on the inside, but that does not mean we cannot heal those wounds and put the pieces back together, so we can be the best person we can be, so we can live a passionate, so we can raise resilient and empowered children for generations to come.

11
Core Love Blueprint Tendencies

In chapters 1 – 5 I introduced the four different types of traits and characteristics that are affected by genetics (nature) and epigenetics (nurture). In chapter 6 I linked genetics and epigenetics to energetic genes and then in chapters 7 – 10 we learned how to deal with the negative emotional tendencies that we were more prone to based on our temperament.

Now what?

Can healing your inner child be that simple?

Is it just possible to create robust family bonds and raise empowered children who will in turn raise empowered families just by releasing the negative emotional tendencies that we either inherited or acquired in our life?

I do not think so.

Yes, identifying core emotional tendencies, working on them, and releasing them from our psyche and energetic body is absolutely necessary to healing the child within and training us to be parents by parenting ourselves first and foremost. I would also argue that it is the first step to healing the child within, but we need to take yet another step in the parenting direction which will become extremely valuable and handy when we have our own children.

I do not believe any healing will be complete without love, and not just any type of love. Healing will never take place without unconditional love and forgiveness. I am a big believer in unconditional love and that it is the way to heal ourselves and others around us. Connecting emotionally through love with others around us will be the best way to build strong relationships, have healthy family culture and raise empowered children.

The power of love is real. The power of love is magical, and it is not only present in dreams and fairy tales. I am introducing the concept of core love tendencies in this chapter as a way for the reader to understand his own love language, his spouse, children, and co-workers so the reader's life will be filled with loving healing energy which will strengthen all kind of relationships.

In my Qigong healing studies, I loved in particular one of the healing techniques in which the practitioner removes negative emotion and negative stored memory from the cells in the body after which he fills the cells with the Divine White Light Energy. Replacing these negative energies with a higher positive vibration ensures the body vibrates at a higher frequency and fills the void the negative energy will leave after it is removed. Due to the nature of things and that it takes time to change any negative energetic pattern, if the practitioner did not replace the negative pattern with a positive pattern, the body would revert to its old energetic pattern.

Wow. What a profound principle and what a brilliant master that understood the power of the Divine and positive energy in maintaining a healthy vibration. The white light has the highest vibrational energy and so is Love's vibrational energy. Doesn't it then make sense to apply the same principle to healing the child within as to healing negative emotions?

This is exactly what I am talking about here. After all, isn't that what parenting being all about? Being a parent is to love, care, raise and look after your child. Doesn't it then make sense that we start to learn how to be better parents by first starting to learn how to parent the child within? To love, care, and look after the child that we have forgotten about all these years. The child we forgot to protect because we were occupied with what others, cultures, religions, politics, and societies told us to do. If this was not child abuse, I do not know what else it could be. If we reverse this pattern and start loving the neglected child within, maybe then and only then when the time comes to have our own children we will never abandon them, abuse them, nor neglect them because we are already parents. Once a parent always a parent no matter what but the secret to be a loving, compassionate and an amazing parent is to first heal our own inner child.

When we get married or when we have children no one hands us a manual on how to be the best partner or the best parent we can be. No one ever tells us what it takes to be a parent and, definitely, no one tells us that by giving birth to a child, we are giving away a piece of our soul to this new soul we are bringing to earth. If someone told us that, then I am pretty sure parents would take better care of the souls they give birth to. They will nourish them, cherish them, protect them, and raise them to be empowered, emotionally balanced, and spiritually aligned so they can pass on this legacy to future generations. If only we had that awareness, things will be different. It is our responsibility as parents to first parent our inner child so we can build stronger family bonds and raise empowered children that will in turn populate earth with higher consciousness and positive vibration to spread peace and love around.

If Malcolm just knew that neglecting his inner child made it easier for him to neglect and give up his own children and family, he might have tried to change things. Malcolm did not learn how to be a parent to his inner child so how do you expect him to be a parent to his born children? He failed his preparatory test to be a parent and then failed it again when he abandoned his children later in life.

Malcolm allowed anger and hate to burn his heart and soul and it blinded him. His anger erupted into rage and its fire burnt his heart slowly, piece by piece, to the point he did not know how to be a parent anymore. Malcolm thought that by punishing his spouse and children he could teach them a lesson on defying his authority and getting out of his control, but instead he punished himself in the process. Eventually, his anger energy affected his heart's energy. He lost joy in life, he was feeling depressed, suffered from high blood pressure and heart disease until one day he dropped dead following a heart attack. He died alone in his one-bedroom apartment in his home town with no friends or relatives around him.

What a loss. Malcolm was a smart proud man who had exceptional leadership skills that could have made him successful in life and in business had he parented his inner child. Malcolm did not know how to love unconditionally, he did not know how to love his own inner child, let alone how to love and take care of his children.

We can all learn from Malcolm's story no matter what our temperament is. Negative emotions can throw us off balance and eventually can kill us if we do not recognize that energy and move it completely out of our body and energetic field. We must consider the body as one unit, one giant cell that if any part of this cell is affected the rest of it will be affected accordingly. Thus, any single negative emotion that escapes our consciousness surveillance will grow uncontrollably until it takes over the whole cell and eventually the cell will suffocate and die due to lack of oxygen and nutrients and due to excess waste and carbon dioxide.

One of my favorite healing exercises ever is the practice of forgiveness. No matter what emotion we are feeling, practicing forgiveness, as hard as it is, will cleanse all these emotions like the rain that falls and washes dirt away. There are many ways to practice the forgiveness exercise, but I am going to give you my favorite way of doing it, which does not involve the presence of the other party. In most cases, you may not be able to be in the presence of the person you want to forgive, either due to them passing away or to your inability to face them. It does not matter if that individual is in front of you or not because at the end of the day, you are doing the forgiveness exercise to release the negative energy and to heal yourself.

The Forgiveness Exercise

This exercise is an amazing practice in allowing you to release any negative energy, especially anger. You may need hours to days to complete it. Be patient, kind and gentle with yourself. The purpose of the exercise is not to make you more resentful about what happened in the past, it is about helping you move through this negative emotional energy. If you want to do it all in one sitting, then by all means, please go ahead and do it. If you want to break it down to smaller chunks of time, that will work too as long as you do it on consecutive days and commit to it and to its completion. Do not start it if you cannot commit to completing it within few days. Schedule a time to practice this exercise when you have the time to do so.

- a- Sit in a quiet place where you know you cannot be interrupted. Have a piece of paper and pen handy for you to use as you progress with the exercise.
- b- Close your eyes and take few deep breaths in through the nose, out through the mouth.

c- Keep your eyes closed and in your mind go through your life starting with childhood and see the people you are angry at.
d- Stay in that space for as long as you need to.
e- Feel the emotions that are coming up and acknowledge them. No blaming. No judging. All you are trying to do here is to acknowledge the anger emotional charge and the source of this energy.
f- Now you can open your eyes and start jotting down the names of the people that you need to forgive.
g- In front of the name of that person write down your emotional charge based on a scale of 1 to 10 with 1 least anger and 10 most anger.
h- Once you are done with your list and rated your emotion toward each person, start by forgiving the people with the least scores (see step i). Since the emotional charge attached to the energy with the lower scores is not enormous it is usually easier to start there first to release this energy. This small success in shifting your energy will make you feel

> like you have accomplished something rather than not being able to forgive and feel like a failure.
>
> i- For each person on your list say the following: "I accept you the way you are. I forgive you and let you go". Short, yet powerful.

Practicing forgiveness was one of the most profound healing exercises I have ever done. When I sat down in that café one morning in March, I released all anger energy from my psyche. It took me hours and hours, sitting in the same chair and I did not leave until I was done forgiving all those who had hurt me, intentionally or unintentionally, in my life. So many emotions surfaced, feeling resentment, anger, betrayal, being taken advantage of.

Final thoughts on healing with love. As we have several core temperaments that result in core emotional tendencies, these temperaments can result in core love tendencies. Each temperament expresses and perceives love differently and to meet your partner's or children needs for love, you must be able to speak their language and keep their love tank full. Love is the food of the *Soul*, so what are you feeding? Your *Soul* and your family *Soul*? How do you show them love and what type of love you are giving them?

We all need to be loved and to feel loved, that is another innate trait in us. The most important part of our relationships is making others feel loved and not only know that they are loved. There is a difference between the two. A child knows that their parents love him, but he may not feel loved, hence, as parents we must ensure that our children feel loved so we can connect with them emotionally and build strong connections that will last for generations to come.

The question now is how you can make others feel loved? Do we all express the same need and in the same way or even in the same intensity? Definitely not. For example, Influencers depend heavily on feeling things so praising them as a way of showing love may not work for them and they may still not feel loved. Thus, give an influencer child a hug or play with them physical games that involves touch. Influencers are more kinesthetic, so touch will have a greater effect on them, especially because they value intimacy. On the other hand, the observer thinker appreciates words of affirmation and encouragement. If you have a thinker child in your family, show them love by encouraging them and by praising them on a job well done. The Doers will love you if you do things for them. Doers don't do well with emotions so saying I love you all day long to a Doer will not make him feel loved but doing the dishes, or putting laundry away will speak volumes with them and will make them feel loved enormously. And finally, the Supporters. Supporters need to feel appreciated at all times. You can show them love by appreciating their efforts and spend quality time with them. They are givers by nature, and want to be allowed the opportunity to support others and give love. Therefore, they will highly appreciate it if you can give them some private and high-quality time to connect with them and have them recharge their batteries.

Finally, no matter what your temperament, the key to having successful and loving relationships is to listen to what your partner or child is saying to you. Their words will reflect their needs so be attentive and listen not only with your ears but with your heart and soul.

Epilogue

When I finished writing this book and started talking to people about it, I was surprised with the response. Once I mentioned the title of the Book "Make Up Don't Break Up" people looked at each other and said, "Break Up". I asked why "Break Up" and not "Make Up"? The answer I always received was look around you. Don't you see how many broken families are around you? The conversation all of a sudden turned into giving me examples of couples who recently broke up with each other for one reason or another.

These conversations only confirmed the necessity of having this book out there to provide direction to the readers and help them mend their relationships. There are so many books on the market that talk about relationships, and this book is not just another one. This book is all about bringing awareness to healing ourselves first, to fix the relationship with ourselves before we seek relationships with others. If I accomplish that, then I have succeeded in shedding some light on how to heal our relationships and make a small dent in the relationships concept.

Men I talked to blame women for the break up and women I talked to blame men for the break up. What if we stop for one second and stop blaming each other? What if we start taking responsibility for our decisions and actions? No relationship ever ends abruptly. The signs are there, and they were there right from the beginning. The truth always reveals itself to us, however, it is us that choose to ignore it. I met many people who came to me talking about their relationships and when I try to help them work on the family dynamic, I always face a brick wall. A wall that was built slowly over years of miscommunication, anger, sadness, and fear, which led to resentment and giving hope on the relationship. At that point, people stop trying to fix the relationship and settle for living in dysfunctional relationships because it is easier to keep the status quo rather than stepping outside of the comfort zone. Feelings are numbed, emotions are absent, partners are not happy where neither of them is willing to approach the other differently to MAKE UP the relationship rather than BREAK UP the relationship.

What in the end breaks up a relationship is one partner giving up on the relationship and stops working on it. This unwillingness to fix what is broken is ultimately what is killing us on the inside and keeps us in this hostile energy of dysfunctional relationships which will eventually result in dysfunctional family dynamics and raising children who do not try their best to reach their fullest potential. This will eventually weaken our society and create mediocracy that will kill excellence not only in our relationships, but in every aspect of our lives.

When I started my healing journey, my mentors always said that healing is like peeling an onion. You peel one layer only for another layer to surface. Over the years of my practice I helped my clients deal with deep seated emotions. We deal with fear only for anger to surface after we heal our fears. We deal with anger only for us to work on healing our sadness.

    Can you imagine how many layers of the onion we must peel before reaching the core?

Epilogue

Can you imagine how many layers of emotions we must peel before we get to the core of our being? What if we got it wrong all along? What if we reverse the process and start healing from the core and work our way out to the surface? Don't you think that is more effective, and will get us faster to where we want to be? I believe it is. So, today, let us work on our core temperaments, core emotions, core needs, core believe systems, and core love to heal the whole being and with it we can heal future generations. Let us work on healing our inner child to heal our relationships so we can MAKE UP and DON'T BREAK UP.

Bibliography

Champagne, F. A., & Mashoodh, R. (2009) 18(3). Genes in context. Current Directions in Psychological Science, 127–131

Goldsmith, H. H., Buss, A. H., Plomin, R., Rothbart, M. K., Thomas, A., Chess, S. Hinde, R. A., McCall, R. B. (1987). Roundtable: What is temperament? Four approaches. Child development, 505-529.

Huizink, A. (2012). Prenatal influences on temperament. In M. Zentner & R. L. Shiner (Eds.), Handbook of temperament (pp. 297–314). New York: Guilford.

Roberts B.W., DelVecchio, W. F. (2000) Jan; 126(1). The Rank-Order Consistency of Personality Traits from Childhood to Old Age: A Qunatitative Review of Longitudinal Studies. Psycol Bull, 3-25

Rothbart, M. K., Sheese B. E., Rueda, M. R. , and Posnerv, M. I. (2011) Apr: 3(2). Developing Mechanisms of Self-Regulation in Early Life. Emot Rev, 207-213

Saudino, K. J., & Wang, M. (2012). Quantitative and molecular genetic studies of temperament. In M. Zentner & R. L. Shiner (Eds.), Handbook of temperament (pp. 315–346). New York: Guilford.

About the Author

Raja Mishal, *PhD* is a Canadian Transformational Speaker, Author, and Trainer. She is a ACPI Certified Core Temperament Coach, a Parent-Family Consultant,  and an Energy Medicine Expert. Her passion is to support families create strong family bonds and meaningful relationships that will last for generations to come. She is the author of "Shift to Shine: Bridging Science and Intuition", and the forthcoming book "Hope Rises: The Power of Taking Action".

She is a graduate of the Medical School at Dalhousie University in Halifax, Nova Scotia, Canada. Her doctoral thesis was in the fields of Molecular Biology, Molecular Genetics, and Neurobiology which earned her two National awards for her research work. As a

About the Author

Neuroscientist, her research focused on understanding how neurons in the brain make connections during early stages of development. Little did she know then that her research work has paved the way for her work today.

In her book "Shift to Shine: Bridging Science and Intuition", Dr. Raja offered a new approach to dealing with stress based on her own personal experience growing up in the Middle East, training as a molecular geneticist and as an energy healing expert. She provided a 3-simple step system that helps individuals explore the energetic root cause of stress and offer strategies to help heal family and personal relationships.

Today, Raja is on a mission to help working professional parents avoid the very same challenges she went through, so they can create strong family bonds and meaningful relationships that will help them reach their full potential in life and shift their legacy for generations to come.

www.ingramcontent.com/pod-product-compliance
Lightning Source LLC
LaVergne TN
LVHW051506070426
835507LV00022B/2955